WORLD ECONOMY EXPLAINED

Insurance

Sean Connolly

amicus

Published by Amicus
P.O. Box 1329
Mankato, MN 56002

Printed in the United States of America, at Corporate Graphics
in North Mankato, Minnesota.

Library of Congress Cataloging-in-Publication Data
Connolly, Sean, 1956-
  Insurance / by Sean Connolly.
    p. cm. -- (World economy explained)
  Includes index.
  Summary: "Explains the functions and history of insurance and its involvement with
  the 2007 credit crunch"--Provided by publisher.
  ISBN 978-1-60753-078-7 (hardcover)
  1. Insurance--Great Britain--Juvenile literature. 2. Insurance--Juvenile literature.
3. Financial crises--Great Britain--Juvenile literature. 4. Financial crises--Juvenile
literature. 5. Credit--Great Britain--Juvenile literature. 6. Credit--Juvenile literature.
I. Title.
  HG8597.C647 2011
  368.00941--dc22
                                                                    2009028004

Designed by Helen James
Edited by Mary-Jane Wilkins
Picture research by Su Alexander

Photograph acknowledgements
Page 7 Gideon Mendel/Corbis; 9 English School/Getty Images; 10 Vittore Carpaccio/
Getty Images; 12 Farrell Grehan/Corbis; 15 Ramin Talaie/Corbis; 16 Susana Vera/
Reuters/Corbis; 17 Ami Green/Getty Images; 19 Paramount/The Kobal Collection;
22 John James/Alamy; 25 Getty Images; 27 Hulton-Deutsch Collection/Corbis;
29 Reuters/Corbis; 30 Eric C. Pendzich/epa/Corbis; 32 Jim West/Alamy;
34 Mike Segar/Reuters/Corbis; 37 Bernd Settnik/DPA/Corbis; 38 Reuters/
Corbis; 40 Despotovic Dusko/Corbis; 42 Wu Hong/epa/Corbis
Front cover Roger Ressmeyer/Corbis

DAD0039
32010

9 8 7 6 5 4 3 2 1

Contents

Looking after Possessions

People have always wanted to look after and protect what they own—their home, furniture, car—even their money. Any of these things can be burned, lost, stolen, or damaged, sometimes in an instant. One way to guard against such losses is to insure them.

Many people pay a regular sum of money to insurance companies to protect their possessions. They also need to report accurately how much the goods are worth. Then if something is lost, stolen, or damaged, the insurance company gives people who have an insurance policy with them money to replace it. Most insurance policies protect buildings, their contents, and cars.

Insurance goes far beyond simply paying to replace damaged or destroyed goods. People can insure against losing their job, becoming ill, or having a vacation canceled because a company goes out of business. One of the most important branches of the insurance industry is life insurance: companies offering this type of insurance pay sums of money to a person's family if he or she dies.

A Crucial Role

The insurance industry does more than offer people peace of mind. It acts as a cornerstone of the world economy, enabling people who make large purchases to protect the items they buy with insurance policies.

As more people buy cars, houses, furniture, and go on more vacations, more jobs are created and protected. Without the protection of insurance, people might feel that these purchases are too risky, so they would buy less, which would result in fewer jobs all around. The world of insurance affects us in other ways. One branch of insurance, called reinsurance (see page 39) actually insures the insurance companies themselves—in case they have to pay out more than they can afford at one time. Governments can also use their money as a form of insurance to protect areas of the economy that are faltering. The U.S. government developed just such a strategy to help the troubled banking industry in early 2009.

Long Tradition

The idea of insurance goes back thousands of years, but the modern insurance industry developed in Britain about 350 years ago. Since then, it has grown and prospered, helping to promote a wider and more international industry. Today, insurance is one of the world's most important service industries, providing countless jobs and generating trillions of dollars worldwide.

Family members wade through their flooded home in northern England in 2007. British insurance companies faced a large number of claims during one of the wettest summers on record.

Setting the Scene

The purpose of insurance is to guard against loss. Many people today understand the need to protect their valuable possessions, such as cell phones, MP3 players, and cars. Most are expensive to replace, and people have to work hard to afford them. But people have owned valuable goods—and wanted to protect them—for hundreds or even thousands of years.

Ancient people may not have used the term insurance, but they often found ways to avoid the risks that might endanger their possessions. The Code of Hammurabi, a record of laws written in Babylon around 2100 BC, describes what we now call insurance. Under the code, traders could take out a loan before their caravan began a long journey across deserts and mountains. If the caravan didn't arrive because the goods were destroyed by storm or stolen, the trader kept the money. If the caravan arrived safely, the trader would repay the loan. The ancient Chinese and Indian civilizations had similar systems to protect their traders.

Although the early insurance arrangements of ancient Babylon and ancient Europe concentrated on shipping, people found ways to minimize risks in many other areas. The inhabitants of some neighborhoods in ancient Rome paid a fee to ensure that a fire brigade would be summoned if a fire broke out. Other Romans paid money to burial clubs, which covered the costs of a burial. Medieval guilds took responsibility for many of the expenses their members faced, looking after their families in times of illness and even paying ransom money to pirates.

Taking to the Seas

The first arrangements that were like those of today's insurance industry also developed through trading deals, although these concentrated on shipping. The ancient Greeks, and the Romans after them, used systems of lending money to sea traders called bottomry. Some of these loans, like those in Babylon, were only repaid if a ship arrived safely at its destination. European sea trade operated under this type of protection system for centuries, long after the fall of the Roman Empire in the fourth century AD.

Over time, bottomry arrangements became more detailed. Travelers—and traders—found land routes slow and dangerous. Even taking into account the risk of storms and pirates, shipping was a safer and more efficient way of carrying trading goods. Some European ports, such as Venice, Pisa, and Genoa became rich and powerful because of their shipping industries.

This engraving, called "Our Desert Camp," shows the hardships that desert travelers faced in the 1800s.

Lawyers and traders in these ports found ways to insure ships and their goods. By the fourteenth century, some of these contracts became standard business practice for their traders. Repaying the cost of a single ship and its cargo was enormous, so it was usual for more than one person to share the risk (and possible cost) of a payout. These people wrote their names under the wording of a shipping contract. The insurance industry still uses the name underwriter to describe someone who takes on some or all of the risk of an insurance contract.

This sixteenth-century religious painting gives a picture of a bustling European port (probably Venice), where ships arrived with precious and exotic goods.

The Modern Era

Another great shipping power, England, was where insurance became a thriving industry, with standard documents and agreed upon working practices. These included the amounts charged, the methods of calculating risk, and the ways in which both the insurer and the insured were protected as much as possible. London in the late seventeenth century was one of the busiest cities in the world, with a growing shipping business. Much of this business was conducted in coffeehouses. Merchants, ship owners, and underwriters would gather in Edward Lloyd's coffeehouse on Tower Street. Lloyd was not involved with insurance directly, but he provided information on shipping that others found helpful in their insurance business.

Lloyd's soon became the most famous center for insurance in England—and the world. The name Lloyd's still stands for insurance in many people's minds, although Lloyd's has never been an insurance business. Just as the stock market is not a business, but a place to buy and sell shares, Lloyd's has always been a center for doing insurance business.

Other companies were formed from the eighteenth century onward, and the insurance industry became more and more varied and competitive. The new companies began to move into areas beyond shipping or even transportation. Some specialized in areas such as fire or life insurance. Others offered insurance coverage for many types of risk. The door had been opened for the insurance industry as we know it today.

EXAMINATION CLOSER EXAMINATION *CLOSER EXAMINATION* CLOSER EXAMINATION CLOSER

The First Insurance Contract?

Many historians believe that the earliest surviving insurance contract is an Italian document that is more than 650 years old. Despite the age of the document, it is not hard for readers today to understand the major elements in this extract, which gives the date, the name of the insurer, the person receiving the insurance, the amount of money, and the length (or term) of the contract: "23rd October 1347 whereby Giorgio Leccavello insures Bartolomeo Basso for the sum of 107 Genoese lire on a cocca [a type of merchant vessel] named *S. Clara* for a voyage from Genoa to Majorca within the term of six months."

A Risky Business

Banking is based on the basic principle of interest. This is the extra money that borrowers pay to banks when they repay a loan, or the money that a bank pays savers for keeping their money deposited in the bank. Banks charge more interest on their loans to borrowers than they pay to savers, which is how they make their money.

The core idea of the insurance industry is the notion of risk. Every insurance agreement, called a policy, guards the insured person against one or more risks that must be clearly stated if the policy is to work properly.

Insurance premiums for hang gliding and other high-risk activities are high because injuries are common.

Into the Pool

Insurance offers people a way to share (or pool) certain risks.
For example, it would be devastating if lightning struck a house
and it caught fire, burning to the ground. Losing a house to lightning
is therefore a serious risk. On the other hand, very few houses are ever
struck by lightning. So homeowners have two conflicting thoughts:
"How awful if that happened to our house" and "Oh well, it probably
won't ever happen to us."

If a cautious homeowner decided to set aside money to rebuild
a house after a lightning strike, the amount needed would be huge.
Homeowner's insurance offers that person the chance to pool the risk
(of a lightning strike) with other homeowners. This pooling could
be done by the owners themselves—if thousands of them put money
into a fund that could be used if lightning struck any of their houses.
Organizing such a fund and collecting regular contributions would
be a real burden, though.

The insurance business works on this principle. People pay a sum
of money, called a premium, to an insurance company as part of their
side of the contract known as the insurance policy. As long as they
have paid the premium and have given accurate information about
what is covered under the policy—a house, personal possessions,
a car, etc.—they will be paid for a repair or replacement.

This arrangement suits both parties in the contract. The individuals
who take out a policy know that their premium is likely to be far
less than the cost of rebuilding a house after a lightning strike,
for example, or the cost of replacing a freezer of food which has
thawed during a power outage. But insurance companies operate as
businesses, so they need to collect more money in premiums than
they pay out for claims.

A Starring Role

One of the most famous insurance underwriters was the renowned English astronomer Edmond Halley. In 1693, Halley developed the first mortality table—calculating the likelihood that a person would die at a certain age. The work was based on statistics from the city of Breslau (now known by its Polish name, Wroclaw). This information was a breakthrough because it enabled companies to work out life insurance premiums accurately for the first time. For example, a 60-year-old is more likely to die than a 20-year-old, so the older person's premium should be higher to reflect this greater risk.

Judging the Odds

Getting the balance right—working out a premium that is attractive to potential customers while still being high enough to make a profit —is a complicated business. This is where insurance underwriters play such an important role. They examine statistics and other evidence to calculate risk. Insurers use their calculations to work out our premiums. If a house is in an earthquake zone, such as California, then the higher risk of earthquake damage would lead to a higher premium. Underwriters also decide on the sort of information that customers should provide, for example, most health insurance policies require details of a person's medical history.

Examining statistics to calculate insurance premiums is not all dry and dusty. Lloyd's of London, which is still the most famous insurance meeting place in the world, has witnessed some very unusual insurance policies. Singer Tina Turner has insured her legs, rock guitarist Keith Richard has insured his fingers, and singer Céline Dion has insured her vocal cords. Lloyd's is also rumored to be working out details of policies to insure space travelers with Richard Branson's Virgin Galactic Company.

Opposite: this model of Virgin Galactic's Spaceship Two *shows the design of the first aircraft planned to take paying passengers across the boundary into space.*

Personal Account
A HELPING HAND

Nina Taylor is a supermodel with a difference. She is a hand model—her graceful hands have appeared in magazine articles, advertisements, and television commercials for leading companies such as Louis Vuitton and L'Oréal. She has even been a hand double for supermodels such as Kate Moss. Nina has to take great care of her hands and avoid accidents such as burning them ("in hand modeling, a lot of powerful lights are used for close–ups and they can get very hot"). A broken nail is more than a hassle—it could mean losing an important job. For peace of mind, Nina has turned to insurance: "I've just insured my hands for a seven-figure sum, which gives some indication of the model fees involved."

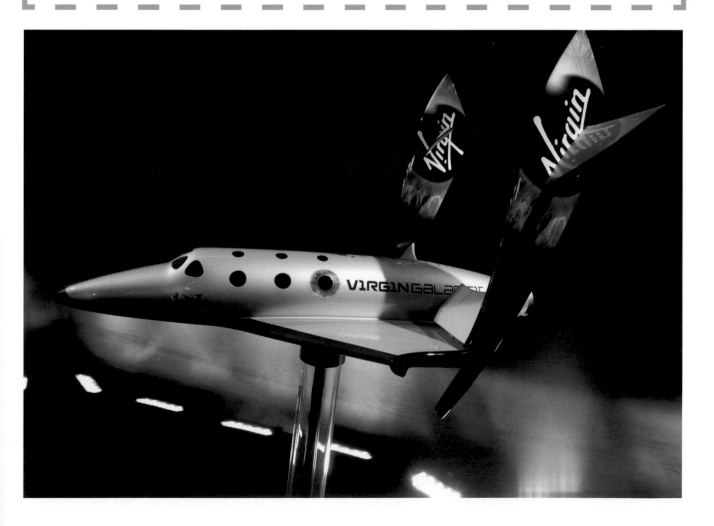

The Market for Insurance

The world has become far more complicated and busy since the foundations of modern insurance industry were laid at Lloyd's coffeehouse in London. Today's insurance policies cover a huge variety of goods, services, and people. Some policies would have baffled seventeenth-century coffee drinkers, such as those covering lost cell phones, flight cancellation insurance, freezer protection, and credit cards.

Today we can apply for insurance coverage by phone and via the Internet, and pay by these methods as well. But despite the new developments always in progress, insurance is still conducted as a business. And those first commercial insurers have left a legacy: Lloyd's is still seen as the heart of the international insurance industry.

Passengers wait to board rescheduled flights at Madrid Airport after a snowstorm closed the airport. Travel insurance policies pay customers if their flight is delayed for a long time or canceled.

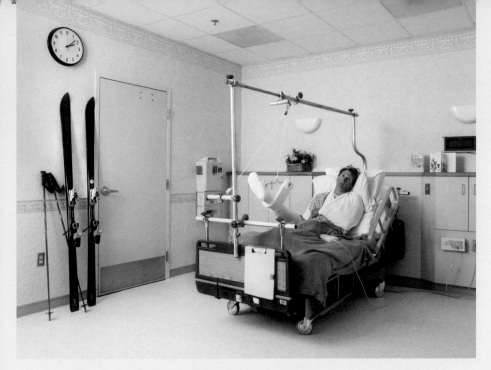

Claims for injuries sustained while skiing—such as a broken leg—are common under travel insurance policies.

Down to Basics

Despite all the developments in the insurance world, the industry is still based on a number of basic principles. For example, even the most up-to-the-minute policy, such as cell phone coverage, still takes into account all kinds of risks. Some of these might be unknown to many people, but they could lead to losses worth thousands or even millions of dollars.

Although there are many varieties of insurance available, most fall into one of two main categories. The first main group is called pure protection insurance. This type includes life insurance, critical illness insurance, and income protection insurance. In each case, the policy-holder is insuring a process or action—such as health, earning power, or even life—rather than an object.

The second category is called general insurance. This type of insurance is much more wide-ranging. After all, people have valued their lives, health, and power to earn for thousands of years. It is only relatively recently that most people have had possessions valuable enough to protect with insurance policies. General insurance is therefore the category that is changing fast as insurers keep pace with the changing needs and demands of modern life. If someone wanted

EXAMINATION *CLOSER EXAMINATION* **CLOSER EXAMINATION** *CLOSER EXAMINATION* CLOSER

Your Money or Your Life

Life insurance is one of the few types of insurance that does not usually benefit the policyholder. Most life insurance policies pay an agreed sum of money after the policyholder has died or developed a serious or terminal illness. These policies provide peace of mind for the person who takes out the policy.

People who are married want to make sure that their spouse will not suffer financially when they die. And once people have children, the life insurance policies become even more attractive. A large lump sum, payable on the policyholder's death, can provide the funds to educate children or to help them set up home on their own. Unfortunately, the idea of a large amount of money being released when someone dies is also tempting for dishonest people. Insurers check the circumstances of a policyholder's death carefully, to make sure that no one who might gain from a life insurance policy played a part in the death. This might seem far-fetched, but many people have been sent to prison for murder because they were the beneficiaries of life-insurance policies.

A famous film called *Double Indemnity* was inspired by just such circumstances. In it, a rich woman persuades a weak young man to kill her husband, making the death look like an accident. The title comes from a clause in some life-insurance policies under which the insurer pays double the normal amount (the indemnity) in certain cases of accidental death.

to insure an MP3 player, the policy would fall into the category of general insurance.

Because so many categories of general insurance—such as cell phone coverage—are relatively new, customers often shop around for the best deals on premiums. That is because insurers might disagree on how great a risk really is in these new areas of business. And as risk is linked to the amount people pay, the premiums can vary along with these different opinions.

The murderers stage a fake accidental death for their victim in the film Double Indemnity.

YOUR MONEY'S WORTH

No-Fault Insurance

Most countries have laws which state that car drivers must take out insurance. After a car accident, insurance companies traditionally agree which driver was responsible (or at fault) for the accident. That driver's insurer then pays for repairs to both cars.

This system operates in many parts of the world. But some countries have a "no fault" system, under which an insurer pays only the repair costs of its customer. If a driver is at fault, then his or her insurer charges them a higher premium because they are a greater risk. Which system do you think is better? Why?

Plain English?

Although the idea of insurance is simple to understand, people in the industry tend to use many unfamiliar technical terms. Insurers point out that life is complicated, so they need to be prepared for any complication that might arise from a claim. And to do that, their work has to be based on some basic principles.

Many basic insurance terms are explained in the glossary (see pages 44–45) and some of the fundamental principles are explained below. Most insurance experts believe that these six concepts are the most important legal principles in insurance.

Insurable Interest

An insurance policy is not legally valid unless the person taking it out has the "insurable interest," or the legal right to insure. In other words, the person must own or otherwise legally control whatever is insured.

Utmost Good Faith

The term "good faith" implies honesty and willingness to provide true and accurate information. An insurance company must act in good faith in the wording of its policies, and customers must also act in good faith. For example, they must provide—or be willing to provide—full details of their insurance history.

Material Facts

Customers must also provide "material facts"—this is information that affects either the risk involved or the amount to be paid out. Material in this sense refers to whether some information has a particular bearing on a policy or a claim. Material information might include whether the insured item is fragile or secondhand, or whether it needs special storage, and so on.

Proximate Cause

This legal term describes exactly how a loss took place. Some types of loss—for example, deliberate breakages—are not covered by insurance policies. The person making the claim must give a full and accurate account of the loss.

Indemnity

This term goes to the heart of how insurance works. The word "indemnify" means to make whole again, and that is what insurance policies do. The indemnity is therefore an agreed amount that will restore the insured person to the position he or she was in before making a claim. For example, the repair of a car damaged in a crash is the indemnity. Many policies allow insurers to reduce the indemnity because of wear and tear or for other reasons.

Contribution

No one can claim more than the true amount they have lost in a claim. So if a person has several insurance policies covering the same risk, he or she cannot claim for the full loss against each policy. If the insured person claims full payment from one insurer, that company is entitled to ask for a contribution from the other insurers.

Subrogation

Once an insurer has paid a claim, it can pursue the claim against anyone else who might have caused the loss or damage. For example, a car insurer might pursue the claim against the driver who caused an accident (or his insurer).

YOUR MONEY'S WORTH

What Does It Mean?

Can you think of ways in which some of the industry's terms could be expressed in simpler words? Or do you think that the language has to be complicated to reflect how complicated the risks might be?

Paying Out

Although there are many different types of insurance, most companies operate along similar lines when paying out on a claim. One of the first things companies do is decide whether a claim is justified. They look at this before they work out how much money they need to pay to settle the claim.

For some small claims, this first step is taken over the phone or when the insured person fills out a form detailing how the loss or damage arose. The company might refuse to go any further if, for example,

A damaged wheel remains after the rest of a bike has been stolen. Insurance claims usually involve explaining how the policyholder guarded against such loss or damage.

a front door had been left wide open and a thief stole a purse from the entryway. In the case of health insurance, the company might discover that an insured person is a smoker—although he or she may not have admitted that fact when applying for insurance.

For larger claims on most types of insurance, the company appoints an independent expert (someone not employed directly by the company) to judge whether a claim is valid. This expert is called a claims adjuster. He or she supplies the company with information and evidence, and usually advises on whether to pay the cost of replacement or repair of lost, stolen, or damaged goods. Because the claims adjuster is paid by the insurers, he or she aims to ensure that the company pays out as little as possible. To balance this, some policyholders employ a claims assessor (who is also an expert) to make sure they receive a fair offer of payment from the insurance company.

Increased Risk

Insurance companies aim to make a profit, so paying out money on a claim will make them look again at their relationship with a policyholder. Insurance is based on the assessment of risk: if someone falls victim to burglary, that person might be at greater risk of falling victim to burglary again (for example, because their street is poorly lit) than other policyholders. The greater risk means that the insurance company will probably charge a policyholder who has made a claim a higher premium than policyholders who haven't made a claim when the policy is renewed.

Sometimes an insurance company might decide that the increased risk is too great and they refuse to insure that person again. Or they raise the premium so much that the policyholder decides not to take out insurance at all. Young drivers may experience this refusal if they have an accident soon after passing their driving test.

Personal Account

GETTING BOGGED DOWN

Roger Canavan had taken his 16-year-old son Jim to the 2007 Glastonbury Festival in England. Like others who had driven there, the Canavans left their car in a neighboring field the festival organizers had set aside for parking. As it so often happens in Glastonbury, it began to rain on Friday and continued raining through Sunday night. The Canavans got up early on Monday and trudged through the rain to their car. The parking field was a sea of mud, with cars stuck everywhere.

Local farmers were using their tractors to pull cars from muddy ruts onto the paved road. When Roger noticed one of these tractors towing a car from the opposite side of the field, he stopped to let it make the turn onto the road just in front of his car. But the tractor took the curve too fast, and the car it was towing began to swing wide of the road as the tractor turned onto it. By now cars had pulled up behind Roger, so he could not reverse. Instead he watched in what seemed like slow motion as the towed car slid closer and closer to his own.

"At first I thought, 'Oh no! It's coming straight at Jim' and I reached across to pull him towards me. Then I saw that it was swinging further to the right—in front of Jim but still about to hit the front of the car. That's when I had my second alarming thought: 'insurance claim!' I knew the bill for this would be a nightmare to sort out even though I had done nothing wrong."

Roger was right. Even though all he wanted was to have his car repaired (and the cost covered by insurance) the claim proved complicated. The repair was done within a week, but his insurance company insisted that Roger pay the usual £200 deductible. This is an agreed sum of money which is deducted from the total cost of a claim. This expense was described as an "uninsured loss."

Roger argued that he should not pay this amount, since he was not at fault. But when his car insurance company tried to reclaim the money from the tractor driver's insurance company, they said that it was the towed driver's fault. And that driver's insurance company said the opposite.

Luckily, both companies agreed that Roger was blameless and they eventually paid the cost of his deductible. By that time it was late January, seven months later.

Conditions remained difficult for days after the last band finished playing at the 2007 Glastonbury Festival. Many people found their cars knee-deep in mud—and needed a tow to reach the nearest road.

Insurance in High-Risk Areas

For more than four decades, many Americans living in high-risk areas—who might otherwise have been refused insurance coverage—have still been able to take out insurance policies. Since the 1960s, 32 state governments have provided money for reinsurance plans so that insurance companies will themselves be covered if there are massive claims on policies. Private insurance companies also help to fund these Fair Access to Insurance Requirements (FAIR) plans.

The need for FAIR plans arose in the 1960s, when many inner-city homes and businesses were damaged during riots. Nowadays, most of the people likely to benefit are those who live near coasts that have damaging floods.

New Directions

Industries have to adapt to changing circumstances to compete for business. For example, very few people owned a computer 30 years ago. When personal computers became affordable, families could buy cheaper, faster models. Then it became possible to hook up computers to the Internet. Next, people began using faster broadband and wireless connections. Any company still producing 1980s-style computers would be out of business.

An insurance company also needs to respond to social changes, although perhaps not as quickly as its computer counterpart. Some of its methods remain more or less unchanged. The wording of an insurance policy protecting a new laptop is much the same as the wording of a policy for an older PC from decades ago. And neither policy is very different from policies protecting rum or silk on an eighteenth-century trading ship.

Where the insurance industry has changed, however, is in how it attracts customers, how efficiently it looks after its money, and how it protects itself. As risk is what insurance is all about, the insurance industry can take no chances when protecting itself.

Moving On

For decades people associated insurance with door-to-door salesmen, who visited existing customers to talk about their insurance needs. The "deal"—agreeing to set up or renew a policy—would be done in a living room or over a cup of coffee. Some salesmen would even cold-call, knocking on strangers' doors, hoping to be allowed in to set up new policies.

Nowadays, much of this business is done over the telephone or via the Internet. Some people complain that cold-calling techniques are too aggressive, forcing people to set up policies when they are not quite sure what they need. Most countries insist that new insurance policies have cooling off periods (see page 31), so that new customers can think through their decisions more carefully and even change their minds.

Insurance companies use the money they receive in premiums to make more profit. They assume that incoming funds (premiums) will be greater than outgoing claims payments, and they invest the extra. This investment has drawn the insurance industry into the credit crunch (see pages 34–37), although insurance experts remain optimistic that they can weather this storm.

Personal Account
SLIPPING THROUGH THE NET?

Many countries, such as Canada, the United Kingdom, and France, have some form of national health service that looks after most of their citizens' health needs. The United States has never had such a system, believing that Americans should take out private health insurance policies to cover their health needs. But the cost of these policies has risen—especially for people with existing diseases. Many Americans have no insurance and so they face enormous bills if they become sick.

President Barack Obama has made health-care reform one of his key projects. In the meantime, many Americans live in fear of ill health. Dr. Ana Manilow of Houston, Texas, describes one such family.

"Penny has had a runny nose all 18 months of her life. She goes to day care while Mom works. Dad holds down two jobs. No one has medical insurance. Sometimes her parents pay out of pocket for a doctor close to home; when they're short of cash, they bring Penny to the emergency room. I diagnose Penny with an upper-respiratory-tract infection and try to spend some time educating the parents about the common cold. They will get a bill for this, probably for $150."

Good Track Record

The insurance industry has had to weather its share of storms over the centuries, as a result of its origins in the world of shipping and sea trade. The profound economic downturn at the start of the twenty-first century (see pages 34–37) has already been described as a hurricane, tornado, or whirlwind. But despite the gloom around them, many insurance experts believe that their industry will emerge from the latest crisis just as strong —though maybe looking a little different.

Why do these insiders feel so confident when so many financial experts have been proved wrong in the last few years? Perhaps the reason lies at the heart of the insurance industry. Other financial services base their predictions on what they see, or even what other people feel. Then they offer advice to individuals and companies based on these observations.

While this advice seems sensible in good times, when things go wrong these financial services come unstuck. The insurance industry, on the other hand, is always trying to come to terms with the unknown and the unpredictable. For example:

- What would happen to a skyscraper if a freak hurricane hit New York City?
- How long is it likely to be before the lead singer of a heavy metal band loses his voice?
- How will the world cope when we run out of oil?

The insurance industry has to address such questions as these all the time if it is to survive. Its track record is good in this respect, which is what inspires the confidence many of its leading figures feel about the future. The fact that insurance companies did not suffer as much during the credit crunch as other financial institutions seems to be evidence in the experts' favor.

Office workers in the West African country of Ghana work on U.S. health insurance information. Insurance companies often operate parts of their business in countries which have lower rates of pay.

Off the Rails

People expect business dealings
to be fair, no matter what industry is involved. Both parties should enter an agreement making it clear what they offer, and at the end both should be satisfied that they understand what has been agreed.

For example, a buyer awaiting delivery of a work of art would be furious to open the package to find a copy. She would hardly feel better if the seller told her that the fine print of clause 22.1 of the sales agreement contained the words "or a copy of that work of art."

This example highlights some business practices that have parallels in the insurance industry. A judge would rule a deal invalid if the sales agreement made no mention of a copy possibly being the main item sold. At the very least, the buyer would be able to claim her money

New York firefighters battle a warehouse blaze in May 2006, one of the most serious fires in the city's history. Insurance companies look closely at claims relating to such fires, to make sure that arson is not involved.

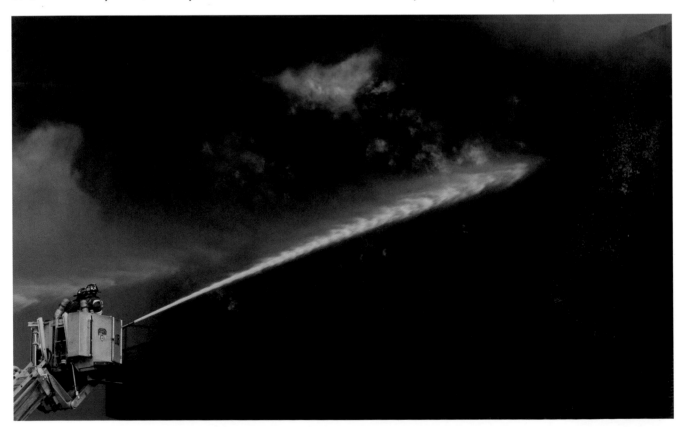

back, and the seller might even be prosecuted. But if a customer finds something unexpected in the small print of a deal, strictly speaking this is not illegal. Instead, it is an example of sharp practice, which damages the reputation of the wider industry.

Sharp Practice

It is rare for an insurance company to be accused of a criminal act. Strict rules, regulations, and codes of practice govern the industry in most countries (see pages 38–39). However, representatives of insurance companies are sometimes accused of sharp practice. Many people take out their first insurance policy through an insurance representative—either in person or on the phone. It is the representative's responsibility to spell out the benefits and drawbacks of any policy. If he or she rushes through this explanation, or phrases it confusingly, then the customer has a chance to reconsider during what's known as a cooling off period. But word of mouth and press reports of such practices can mean that the company's reputation suffers, which may affect its business.

Insurance companies, like other members of the financial industry, are also aware that they can be mocked—and that business may suffer as a result—if their communications seem deliberately confusing or complicated. The Plain English Campaign in the UK is on the lookout for such communications and singles out the worst offenders for its annual Golden Bull awards (see page 33).

Red Lines and Gray Areas

One section of the insurance industry that occupies a gray area is a practice called redlining. The term arose in the United States, where banks, insurance companies, and other financial companies used a red pen to mark out (or redline) some neighborhoods in cities. Some of these neighborhoods had the highest numbers of crimes and large insurance claims. Insurance companies, many Americans argued, responded by making it harder for residents in those neighborhoods

to take out insurance. This practice was hard to prove but it reflected badly on many financial services (including insurance) because the redlined neighborhoods had the highest proportion of ethnic minorities in the cities. Making it impossible—or very difficult—to obtain financial protection broke laws against discrimination.

Some people argue that redlining continues today. They claim that insurance representatives can work out people's ethnic background using clues such as their address, last name, and accent, and then offer them unreasonably high quotes as a way of refusing to do business with them.

Michele and Alexander Baker relax in their New Orleans home after their insurance company paid for massive repairs. Floodwaters from Hurricane Katrina had reached the living room ceiling in August 2005.

Is the Customer Always Right?

When things really go wrong with insurance, it is usually the policy-holders rather than the insurer who is at fault. And other policyholders, who make up the majority of insurance customers, pay for it. Insurance fraud is common, partly because some people believe they won't be caught. Insurance fraud has happened in cases of burned down businesses and homes, and in cases of car accidents. False or exaggerated claims take time to investigate, which is one reason costs can be high. Insurance companies are not charities, so they pass on these extra costs to the other policyholders. The industry is calling for harsher penalties for those convicted of fraud. Only then, they argue, will the cost of fraud to all policyholders be kept down.

Crash for Cash

Thirteen members of a British "crash for cash" gang were found guilty of insurance fraud in August 2008. By making claims for accidents that never happened, the gang received about $400,000. Two brothers, Bobby and Umear Gul, paid others to pretend they had car accidents. They helped them make insurance claims for the fake accidents, even providing false paperwork (for towing and repairs) to back up their claims. The police and the Insurance Fraud Bureau took two years to uncover the truth. They found evidence that the gang had deliberately damaged vehicles in order to claim insurance money for repairs, rental cars, personal injury, and even supposed loss of earnings (because of the time spent filling out insurance claims).

EXAMINATION *CLOSER EXAMINATION* **CLOSER EXAMINATION** CLOSER EXAMINATION CLOSER

Clear as Mud

The following passage was given a Golden Bull Award in 2008 by the Plain English Campaign. It was a response from Scottish Life to a customer's question about how the company calculates the earning power of a policy.

"The growth of the policy is calculated through more than one area of the plan, the annual reversionary bonus is only one area of this growth, the part of the growth rate of this policy is the increased rates of the terminal bonus rate for a policy with a term of 24 years is currently 24 percent of the basic sum assured and the total bonuses attaching. The terminal bonus is only applied at the end of the plan and is not known to ourselves until this is applied."

The Credit Crunch

A saying often credited to ancient China goes: "May you live in interesting times." At first, this seems like a blessing, suggesting that those times will be full of fun and excitement. But on reflection, the same words could be a curse—"interesting" could be a rephrasing of "unpredictable," "risky," or "dangerous." By comparison, times of peace or wealth could be described as uninteresting or dull.

The financial world became very "interesting" in the middle of 2007. In stock markets around the world, there were sudden and dramatic falls in share prices. A healthy stock market is often seen as the symbol of a steady and safe world economy. People and companies alike can invest their money, confident that it will earn money as share prices rise. The sudden fall in 2007 was unexpected, as share prices had been rising steadily for more than ten years.

Opposite: Many people saw the massive fall in share prices on February 27, 2007, as a warning that even worse was to come. This image shows traders at the New York Stock Exchange, where many of those falls were recorded.

The trigger for the abrupt change came from banks, many of which had lent money irresponsibly when times were good. People who had been thought of as bad risks because they suffered from poor health, or were likely to lose their jobs, were given loans to buy houses. Then housing prices began to fall in 2006, and by mid-2007, some of those who had risky loans were unable to repay their banks. Many banks suffered huge losses, and some went out of business. Other banks then became incredibly cautious, making it harder for people to borrow money (or get credit, to use the banking term). And when companies find it hard to borrow money to build their businesses, the wider economy suffers.

Within months, it became clear that the credit crunch extended far beyond its origins in the world of banking. Everyone and everything seemed to be affected. Companies began losing customers and money, which in turn meant they needed fewer workers. As more people became unemployed, and those working worried about the security of their jobs, overall spending went down. One thing led to another, and by 2008 it became clear that the world was facing a recession.

No one could deny that the crisis was global, and experts argued that the solution also had to involve the entire world. With that in mind, the leaders of the 20 richest countries (the G20) met in London in April 2009 to sow the seeds of global recovery. But even their best intentions were affected by disagreements among those countries about how best to end the world recession. Some, such as France, wanted to give governments more power to control financial deals —even those outside their own borders. Others, such as the United States and Britain, argued that the best solution was to pump more money into the world economy to increase trade.

Dealing with the Emergency

The insurance industry is part of the wider financial picture and it has suffered as a result. One obvious way in which insurance companies have been hit is in their own investments. Companies save and invest much of their income. In the case of insurance companies, this comes in the form of the premiums paid by policyholders. And since the crunch began, the value of investments has dropped significantly.

Opposite: Germans looking for work wait outside a government labor office. Even powerful economies have been hit hard by the credit crunch.

More Regulation?

The American insurance industry is not regulated. This means that the government has no control over the insurance industry, and there are no organizations set to regulate or monitor it. Regulations have been proposed before, but have never turned into laws. With the credit crunch of 2007, many discussions have formed around the insurance industry and perhaps starting to regulate it.

William Berkley, chairman of the Board of the American Insurance Association (see page 39 for more detail), testified in March 2009 that he supports putting more regulation into the insurance industry. In his statement to the U.S. Senate, he addressed why regulation inside the insurance industry would be good:

"While property-casualty insurance plays an essential role in our economy, it has been successfully weathering the current crisis. It has had to carefully navigate through some heavy turbulence to do so, but the sector remains strong overall… If this crisis has revealed anything, it is the need for more–not less–regulatory efficiency, coordinated activity or tracking, sophisticated analysis of market trends, and the ability to anticipate and deal with potential systemic risk before the crisis is at hand… It makes little sense to look at national insurance regulation after the event has already occurred, but all the sense in the world to put such a structure in place to help avoid the consequences of an unforeseen event."

Insurance is very unpredictable, but perhaps with more regulation we can be better prepared for what lies ahead. Many proposals have been drawn up, but no laws have been passed yet.

Personal Account

CHECKING FOR DAMAGE

Raj Singh is the Chief Risk Officer of Swiss Re, one of the world's leading insurance companies. In late 2008, he explained why the insurance industry was protected from the worst problems of the credit crunch:

"Financial market conditions like these are unprecedented, and insurers' assets are of course affected. However, we have to remember that this crisis was started by the collapse of credit markets and the freezing of liquidity that followed: this is a big issue for banks, of course, but for insurers, who are largely funded by their policyholders, this is less of an issue. There is a big difference between insurers and banks: our business models are fundamentally different."

Extra Protection

Any industry that combines the unknown (risk) with large amounts of money must have rules and regulations to make sure it operates fairly. Many regulations are aimed at insurance companies themselves, making sure that they present their information clearly, treat policyholders fairly, and behave responsibly and legally.

Other regulations are aimed at policyholders and other insurance customers and these include elements of criminal law (such as fraud, see pages 32–33) that are especially relevant to the insurance industry. Together, these regulations protect the industry and customers alike.

The 9/11 terrorist attack in 2001 led to the largest and most complicated insurance claims in U.S. history. People claimed more than $41 billion in damages.

Finally, the insurance industry has long relied on another method to protect itself—not against dishonest customers but against taking on too much risk at one time. Nearly two thousand years ago the Roman poet Juvenal wrote *"Quis custodiet ipsos custodes?"* which translates as "Who will guard the guardians themselves?" A similar concern runs through the insurance industry. If, for example, a town is flooded and most of the flooded citizens have insured their property with the same company, that company might collapse as a result of receiving so many claims at once.

Because of that risk, most insurance companies take out insurance policies of their own, to protect against an onslaught of claims. This extra protection is called reinsurance. A massive disaster, such as the 9/11 terrorist attack in New York City in 2001, can lead to enormous reinsurance claims. But a river bursting its banks in a small town and flooding dozens of houses could be just as devastating for a small local insurer.

Advocating for Insurance

The American Insurance Association (AIA) represents the property-casualty insurance trade industry. It does not act as a regulator body. AIA does, however, act as an advocate for 350 insurance companies on a state and federal level. They take on key issues in the insurance industry, such as asbestos reform and terrorism insurance. AIA members write letters to the government urging them to pass certain bills, and they also publish statements to the media once the bills have been passed. Their influence has had a large impact on the insurance industry by helping insurance companies link together and solve issues that affect them and the customers they serve.

YOUR MONEY'S WORTH

A Good Balance?

Do you think the balance is right between laws and regulations protecting insurance companies against fraud on the one hand, and looking after customers' rights in their dealings with insurers, on the other?

Looking Ahead

Insurers earn their living by minimizing the risks the future brings. So the insurance industry should be able to look ahead with greater accuracy than other types of companies. That is the theory. But even forward-looking industries watching for change can be taken by surprise.

One leading insurance executive noticed that there was just one very old-fashioned computer in her building when she joined the company in 1995. Coming from a banking background where computers were essential, she was shocked. But she noted that within two years, her company had caught up and relied heavily on computing skills. By then the banks where she had previously worked were in a worse financial state than her insurance company during the credit crunch of 2008–09.

Sunflowers wither in dry fields during a prolonged drought in Spain. These conditions are likely to become more familiar in the future, and insurers must plan for the effects of climate change.

Climate Change

In some ways, insurers need to look into crystal balls to predict the future, if they are to protect themselves against risks that otherwise seem unpredictable at present.

As early as 2000, insurers had begun paying out larger than usual amounts for flood-related claims. Many experts, both inside the insurance industry and in the world of science, believed that the floods were the

first evidence of climate change, and that worse was to come.

The Environmental Protection Agency states that the total dollars paid out in natural disaster-related claims since 1990 is 50 percent greater than the losses incurred over the past 40 years combined. Insurance companies are also calling for action to reverse some of the causes of global warming.

That observation sums up the position of the insurance industry. It might seem slow to adapt to change, but it manages risk (of falling behind) and corrects itself. None of this is done rashly, which means that when things go wrong for other industries, insurance is shielded by that same caution and prudence.

Spreading the Word

Consider some of the following facts, which may come as a surprise to many people:

• The American insurance industry is worth $123 billion yearly.
• State Farm, a leading insurance company, wrote more than 78 million policies in 2009.
• The insurance industry had about 2.3 million wage and salary jobs in 2006. Insurance carriers accounted for 62 percent of jobs, while insurance agencies, brokerages, and providers of other insurance-related services accounted for 38 percent of jobs.

With the number of jobs that are available in the insurance industry, it would seem natural that a lot of people would flock to this enormous industry. It seems, though, that the insurance industry has somewhat of an image problem. When people think of a career in insurance, they tend to think of all the negative aspects. They believe insurance involves either crunching numbers in a dull office, or having to explain to the policyholders why they won't receive all the money they've been expecting after a disaster.

While some jobs within the insurance industry do include duties that are challenging in that way, they also include other facets that are interesting and provide a chance to move up the career ladder. There are many different types of jobs within the insurance industry, and not all of them involve selling insurance. An underwriter is one job of

Recent university graduates attend a job fair in Qingdiao, a city in eastern China. Insurance companies seek to attract young people, especially in fast-growing economies such as China's.

Personal Account

TAKING PRIDE IN THE JOB

Annabel Fell-Clark is chief executive of Axa Art, which insures valuable works of art. She feels that her job satisfies all her early ambitions: "I always wanted to be a stuntwoman when

I was little, so if that didn't work it would definitely have to be a career in risk-taking. I find that insurance gives me a good balance of intellectual stimulation, trading, problem solving, and relationship building.

"At the claims end of the process, I find it fascinating trying to get into the psyche (mind) of the client, to see what makes them tick."

many within insurance. Underwriters deal with risk. They decide how often things such as death, sickness, injury, disability, and loss of property occur, as well as the costs of these things. They help design insurance policies that insurance agents will sell.

Insurance investigator is another position. An insurance investigator handles claims when companies suspect fraudulent or criminal activity, such as suspicious fires, questionable workers' disability claims, or hard-to-explain accidents. Investigators carry out background checks on suspects to determine if they have a history of fraud. They then perform inspections that include interviewing the people in question and possible witnesses, and taking photographs. Investigators often consult with legal representatives and are sometimes called to testify as expert witnesses in court cases.

A career in insurance can be very satisfying. As the insurers put it, without insurance there would be less risk taking— less driving, fewer doctor appointments, less shipping, and less business. And more to the point, if they had insurance, poor people would never be left homeless after a natural disaster.

Glossary

assets   Items of value owned by a company or an individual.

beneficiary   The person named in an insurance policy who will receive a payment or other benefits under the policy.

bottomry   Lending money to a sea trader on condition that it is paid back only when the merchant ship arrives safely at its port.

claim   A request for payment from a policyholder to an insurance company.

claims adjuster   A representative of an insurance company who examines a claim to determine how much money should be paid.

claims assessor   A representative of a policyholder who examines a claim to determine whether the insurance company is offering a fair amount of money.

climate change   The gradual rise in Earth's air and sea temperatures, leading to widespread changes in weather, such as more storms and floods.

cold call   An uninvited visit or telephone call from a representative of a company.

cooling off period   A period of time, usually two weeks, during which new customers can reconsider a new agreement (such as an insurance policy) and possibly cancel it.

deductible   The first part of any claim, which must be paid by the policyholder and not the insurer.

discrimination   Unfair treatment because of someone's appearance, religion, etc.

fraud   Dishonestly taking money from a company.

general insurance   The type of insurance that pays a policyholder if an insured item is stolen, damaged, or burned.

gray area   A subject that is neither one thing nor another.

income protection   An insurance policy which pays out if someone loses a regular source of income.

intellectual   To do with the mind and intelligence.

interest   Extra money paid back to a lender (in the case of a loan) or paid to a saver.

life insurance   A policy that pays an agreed sum to beneficiaries when the policy-holder dies.

liquidity (in banking)   A measure of how easy it is for people to borrow money.

loan   Borrowed money that has to be repaid within an agreed period.

pension   A regular source of income once a person stops working regularly.

policy   The official agreement between the insurance company and the customer.

policyholder   The insurance company's customer.

premium   The sum paid to the insurance company under the terms of the policy.

profit   The amount of money made when the return is greater than the amount spent.

prosecute   To bring legal action against an individual or organization.

pure protection insurance   Insurance that covers the risk of death or disability.

recession   A period of severe economic decline, lasting six months or more.

redlining   Singling out areas for tougher treatment.

reinsurance   A type of insurance that protects insurance companies against the risk of enormous payouts.

renewal   The agreement to continue with (renew) an insurance policy.

return   The extra amount (over and above what they paid in) that savers receive at the end of a business agreement.

share   Part ownership of a company, which people can buy or sell.

sharp practice   Business dealings that are not illegal but disadvantage customers.

stock market   The business area where shares are bought and sold.

terminal (of an illness)   Leading to death, with no chance of recovery.

Treasury   A government department that looks after the national economy.

underwriter   An individual or organization that agrees to assume some or all of the risk in an insurance policy in return for some or all of the premium.

wear and tear   Loss in value over time as a result of being used regularly.

Further Reading

The Credit Crunch Colin Hynson (Sea-to-Sea, 2010)

New Global Economies Colin Hynson (Sea-to-Sea, 2010)

What Is Insurance? Carolyn Andrews (Crabtree, 2009)

Web Site Links

Terrorism Insurance Information
http://aiadc.org/aiapub/landing.aspx?m=
2&v=110&docid=308397

Facts on Car Insurance for Teens
http://www.progressive.com/shop/teen-car-
insurance-resources.aspx

International Insurance Fact Book
http://www.internationalinsurance.org

Insurance Basics
http://www.moneyinstructor.com/insurance.asp

Index